WILLIAM WALTON

CONCERTO FOR VIOLA AND ORCHESTRA

Reduction for Viola and Piano

EDITED BY

CHRISTOPHER WELLINGTON

MUSIC DEPARTMENT

OXFORD
UNIVERSITY PRESS

OXFORD
UNIVERSITY PRESS

Great Clarendon Street, Oxford OX2 6DP, England

Oxford University Press is a department of the University of Oxford.
It furthers the University's aim of excellence in research, scholarship,
and education by publishing worldwide

Oxford is a registered trade mark of Oxford University Press
in the UK and in certain other countries

15 17 19 20 18 16 14

ISBN 978–0–19–368131–6

Music origination by Figaro,
Printed in Great Britain on acid-free paper by
Halstan & Co. Ltd., Amersham, Bucks

INTRODUCTION

On the following pages is printed the full Preface to the Concerto for Viola and Orchestra as given in the William Walton Edition volume of this work (vol. 12). This gives full details of the composition and history of this fascinating work. The final sections ('The solo line' and 'The Riddle version') also detail how a major and unfortunate misunderstanding between composer and publisher resulted in the 'wrong' version of the solo part being printed in both the 1962 full score and the piano reduction from 1963 until 2002.

The purpose of this Introduction and the inclusion of the complete Edition Preface is to urge players to follow the form of the solo viola part as printed in this piano reduction. This is the version edited and revised by Frederick Riddle and, it cannot be emphasized too strongly, the form of the solo part chosen by the composer.

Riddle was the soloist in the first recording of the work (issued in 1938), with Walton conducting. Recalling his first impressions of the solo part, Riddle commented 'I looked at it and thought – I can't play from this part; the bowings and articulations don't fit the nature of the music as I understand it.' Hence his thorough revisions, which proved to be very much to Walton's liking and which led to the composer's request they should be published to replace the solo part as first issued.

The present piano reduction was made by Geoffrey Pratley and published in 1993. With a few corrections, it appears here exactly as it did then. The solo line can be played with either orchestration; where markings and tempi differ both are given in this edition, with the 1962 details set in lighter type. Players should bear in mind that these 1962 details originate from an editor, not the composer.

The Walton/Riddle recording has the following tempi:

$$\text{Movt. I} \quad \left.\right. = c.54$$
$$\text{Movt. II} \quad \left.\right. = c.132$$
$$\text{Movt. III} \quad \left.\right. = c.86$$

This was the only recording of which the composer is known to have approved, and in the view of the present editor these metronome marks constitute the most favourable starting-point (of course accepting that soloist and conductor will have their own view).

To conclude with a personal view: in terms of interpretation I suggest that this concerto should not be thought of as an opportunity for virtuoso display and personal invention, but rather as a narrative in which the viola is the leading voice. The nature of that narrative may be related to the composer's frustrated feelings for the dedicatee and the uneasy atmosphere that prevailed between the two world wars, with the pretence of peace illustrated by the concerto's trademark false relations.

CHRISTOPHER WELLINGTON
Southbourne, 2011

PREFACE

To the William Walton Edition volume of the Concerto for Viola and Orchestra

Considering the major effect it was to have in alerting both critics and public to the true stature of William Walton as a composer, the Concerto for Viola and Orchestra had a very uncertain start in life. A perceptive suggestion from Sir Thomas Beecham that he might compose something for the great viola player Lionel Tertis encouraged the 26-year old Walton to start working on a concerto during his annual visit to Amalfi with Osbert Sitwell in the winter of 1928. What was it, we may wonder, about the overture *Portsmouth Point* (1925), *Siesta* (1926), or the Sinfonia Concertante for Orchestra with Piano (1927) that caused Beecham to mention a concerto for Tertis to the young composer?

In the 21st century we are perhaps already too remote in time to realize the standing and reputation of Lionel Tertis (1876–1975) in his prime, but we can learn something from Arnold Bax's appreciation of him, written seven years before the Viola Concerto came into being:

> The technical and emotional capabilities of the viola have been developed in Mr Tertis's hands to a point undreamed of, as I believe, before his time. [He] has extended its possibilities until it has been proved capable of almost all the nuances of the other strings besides that peculiar acrid poignancy which this great artist derives from the higher register of the A string and which no other medium known to me can produce. It must have been in my student days that a prominent British composer remarked to me 'Surely Tertis's viola playing is the best performance on any instrument to be heard in this country'. Time has only justified and solidified this judgement.[1]

In 1964 Tertis was awarded the coveted Gold Medal of the Royal Philharmonic Society, thus achieving a unique confirmation of his eminence; he had progressed from self-taught beginnings through orchestral ranks to ultimate acceptance as a true viola soloist.

A concerto for the viola was a real rarity in the early twentieth century. In his autobiography Tertis wrote, 'When I first began to play the viola as a solo instrument, prejudice and storms of abuse were my lot. The consensus of opinion then was that the viola had no right to be heard in solos … as a student at the RAM [I played] the Mendelssohn and Wienawski D minor concertos (of course a fifth lower but exactly as written for the violin) at two of the fortnightly students' concerts there'.[2] Almost the only acceptable major work for viola with orchestra was Berlioz's *Harold in Italy* (1834). When Fritz Kreisler invited Tertis to play Mozart's Sinfonia Concertante, K364, with him in a 1924 recital (with piano!) at the Royal Albert Hall the work was regarded as a comparative novelty by the London press. Earlier works, like the concertos by Telemann, Stamitz, and Rolla, had yet to be rediscovered. In Britain the early 1900s saw the creation of viola concertos by Cecil Forsyth, J. B. McEwen, and York Bowen, but most of the works for the instrument from this period that have survived in the repertory bear less ambitious titles like Benjamin Dale's Suite, Op. 2, Arnold Bax's extended single-movement *Phantasy*, and Vaughan Williams's *Flos Campi*.

Composition

The progress of the concerto's composition is fitfully chronicled in Walton's letters from Amalfi to his friend and financial supporter, the poet Siegfried Sassoon.[3] On 5 December 1928 he wrote, 'I have been working hard at a Viola Concerto suggested by Beecham and designed for Lionel Tertis'; by 2 February of the following year he was able to report, 'I finished yesterday the second movement of my Viola Concerto. At the moment, I think it will be my best work, better than the "Sinfonia" [Concertante], if only the third and last movement works out well—at present I am in the painful position of starting it, which is always full of trials and disappointments, however I hope to be well away with it in a day or two'. On 12 February Walton could confirm, 'Otherwise I've no news, except that I have started on the third movement and hope to complete it soon.'

The pianist Angus Morrison, who lived very near Walton at this time, received a letter from Amalfi referring to the Viola Concerto which stated, 'My style is changing—it is becoming more melodious and mature'.[4] In a memoir as part of a BBC radio programme Morrison also recalled, 'When very soon after he returned to London the following spring he came and played it to me I realised the true significance of the remark. In this work he had in fact reached complete maturity of style and given full rein for the first time to his entirely personal lyrical gift. To my astonished ears it seemed to me, in spite of his woefully inadequate piano playing, a masterpiece in the real sense of the word'.[5]

Walton acknowledged two influences on the composition of his Viola Concerto: first, Paul Hindemith's *Kammermusik Nr. 5*, for viola and large chamber orchestra (1927), and second, Prokofiev, whose First Violin Concerto (1916–17) shows a similar scheme of movements and the device of returning to the opening material in the closing pages.[6]

When Walton returned to London in the spring of 1929 he sent the completed work to Lionel Tertis who, according to the composer, rejected it by return of post without explanation. This is how Tertis recalled the incident:

> One work of which I did *not* give the first performance was Walton's masterly concerto. With shame and contrition I admit that when the composer offered me the first performance I declined it. I was unwell at the time; but what is also true is that I had not learnt to appreciate Walton's style. The

innovations in his musical language, which now seem so logical and so truly in the mainstream of music, then struck me as far-fetched. It took me time to realize what a tower of strength in the literature of the viola is this concerto, and how deep the gratitude that we who play the viola should feel towards the composer.[7]

It seems likely that the harmonic idiom, with its frequent false relations, looked too modern to him; Lillian Tertis, the great player's widow, remarked that 'Lionel couldn't imagine that a chord containing C♯ and C♮ could possibly sound well'.[8] Walton was so downcast at this rejection that he seriously considered converting the work into a violin concerto, but changed his mind following a suggestion from a valued BBC friend, Edward Clark. Clark knew that Walton and Hindemith (his senior by six years) were already on friendly terms and reminded the disappointed composer that Hindemith was also a well-known viola player, both as soloist and chamber musician; furthermore he was going to be in London at the time of the proposed first performance. Clark arranged to have the score sent to Hindemith and secured his agreement to play the solo part for the first performance.

Following Tertis's initial rejection, Walton abandoned all idea of acknowledging the player at the head of the score and instead dedicated the work 'To Christabel'. Christabel was the Hon. Mrs. Henry McLaren who in 1934 was to become Lady Aberconway when her husband succeeded his father as second Baron. She had long been very friendly with Osbert Sitwell, to whom she remained devoted to the end of his life in 1969, and Walton would have met her regularly at the Sitwells' London house and at the Derbyshire family seat, Renishaw. She was probably the first of his serious romantic attachments, but although the attraction was mutual, the relationship seems to have remained platonic.[9]

Early performances

The première of the Viola Concerto took place at a Promenade Concert at Queen's Hall on 3 October 1929, with Hindemith as soloist and Walton himself conducting the Henry Wood Symphony Orchestra. At the first rehearsal the orchestral parts were found to be notably inaccurate, and Walton sat up through the night correcting and re-writing. Hindemith was dismayed at having so little time to rehearse;[10] he wrote to his wife on 2 October: 'I have just come from the rehearsal (evening around 7); it should have been early this morning but wasn't because other things were being rehearsed ... Walton is conducting the concerto himself. It won't be up to much. So far he has only had one rehearsal in which he managed to play the first movement just once. The orchestra is bad, consisting mainly of women, and English ones at that.'[11]

Part of the concert, which was devoted exclusively to British music, was broadcast on one of the BBC's Daventry transmitters, and this included the concerto. The performance scored an undoubted success; the concerto's lyrical and dramatic elements made a deep impression not only on enthusiasts for contemporary music but on the musical public as a whole. The anonymous critic of *The Times* (almost certainly H. C. Colles) reported on the occasion in these terms:

After the full scoring of the elder composer [Bax], the low scale of tone, partly conditioned, no doubt, by the nature of the solo instrument, made its colour sound a little drab. Once the ear had adjusted itself to the new values, its subtlety, its rhythmic vitality, and its lyrical charm were evident enough. The mastery and the handling of the material chosen and the restraint which has been imposed upon his facility constitute a real and astonishing advance in the composer's development.[12]

In the *Musical Times* Eric Blom was even more enthusiastic:

The success of the Viola Concerto by William Walton might almost be said to have amounted to a sensation, were it not that the music made an impression, not a mere hit. It is one of the most remarkable of recent compositions, British or otherwise, the more so because it does not draw attention to itself by anything but sheer quality.[13]

It is very typical of Walton (with his innate modesty and ironic humour) that he should say 'I knew little of the viola when I started save that it made a rather awful sound', and then proceed to write a concerto which captures the nature of this unusual solo instrument to a superlative degree.

Walton, although extremely grateful to Hindemith for performing at the première, later recalled, 'His technique was marvellous, but he was rough—no nonsense about it. He just stood up and played'.[14] Along with many other viola players, Tertis attended the first performance and reacted similarly. In his autobiography he wrote, 'The notes certainly were all there, but the tone was cold and unpleasing and the instrument he played did not deserve to be called a viola, it was far too small.'[15]

Tertis lost no time in writing to Walton, apologizing for his initial rejection and promising to perform the concerto subsequently. His first appearance with the work was less than a year later, on 4 September 1930, at the ISCM Festival at Liège with the composer conducting. After a further performance that year in Germany, Walton wrote to the concert pianist Harriet Cohen:

The orchestra was bloody, the rehearsals ditto—in fact everything seemed, with the exception of Mr. Tertis, who was a saint and angel throughout—to be all wrong, till at the performance I found myself at the top of my form and behaved like Toscanini and it all went perfectly. If the orchestra had been good the performance could not have been better. It consisted of the professors and students of the Conservatoire the average age of the former being about 90 and the latter about 15. However, they did try and in fact rose a certain distance for the occasion, and the concerto made the hit of the Festival—at any rate so far. The applause—tears—and cheers, couldn't have been better, and Tertis and I were more tired by walking on and off than by playing.

My arm is fatigued by autograph signing and I was touched by the number of orchestral players who asked if I had written concertos for their several instruments. You have no conception what Tertis has made out of the work—if you liked it before, you will just pass out when you hear him play it. I nearly did myself.[16]

Over the next few years Lionel Tertis made handsome amends for his hasty refusal of the first performance, playing the concerto many times. This included appearances in London, Birmingham, Manchester, and Liverpool, as well as a famous 1932 Edinburgh concert when Adrian Boult persuaded his soloist to play the entire concerto again in the second half of the programme.[17] Tertis's performance was broadcast from Zürich and Berne during a BBC Symphony Orchestra tour of Europe with Boult conducting; at least eight broadcasts took place in Britain. It has been calculated that Tertis played the Walton Concerto some 30 times, including a post-retirement appearance on 9 July 1940 at Queen's Hall, shortly before its destruction in the London Blitz.

Publication

The first publication of the Concerto for Viola and Orchestra was by Oxford University Press in 1930, in the form of full score and arrangement for viola and piano. The arranger of the piano reduction was not specified, but was almost certainly Walton himself; the separate solo part that came with it was identical with that shown in the full score. An engraved set of orchestral parts was also produced at about the same time, though never put on sale.

Within two years the OUP music catalogue included an additional item: 'Viola Solo part, edited by Lionel Tertis, obtainable separately. 1s 6d'.[18] In this, Tertis transposed several passages up an octave, or added octave doublings; he also provided his inimitable (and all but unplayable) fingerings. To judge from the great player's personal copy, what Tertis actually played—at least towards the end of his career—showed even wider variations from the composer's text than his printed version.[19]

A wish to modify the solo line also characterized the approach to the concerto adopted by the Scottish viola player William Primrose. The programme note of a Royal Philharmonic Society concert on 27 February 1936, under Beecham, at which he gave his first performance of the work, announced, 'Mr. Primrose's rendering of the solo viola part diverges occasionally from the published version'. On 2 October 1961, while preparing for the publication of the concerto's new orchestration, Walton wrote to OUP, 'William Primrose's version [of the solo part] is yet a 4th! because it differs in many respects—not the actual notes, but bits and pieces have been shoved up an octave or are in octaves, etc. And more often than not with good effect. I was just wondering what Y.M. [Yehudi Menuhin] will do with

it—whether it is worth while sending him an annotated copy incorporating W.P.'s various tricks'.[20]

After hearing Primrose's 1955 recording the conductor Denis Vaughan queried the audible departures from the printed text; in a reply Alan Frank, head of OUP's music department, wrote, 'As far as I can tell William approves of what Primrose does but doesn't come off the fence sufficiently to say that they must all be incorporated in anything we print'.[21]

Recordings

Lionel Tertis was the soloist in a performance at a BBC Symphony Orchestra concert on 24 February 1937, with Ernest Ansermet conducting: the programme also included Berlioz's *Harold in Italy*. The concert marked the player's 60th birthday, and unexpectedly his retirement. Tertis had been troubled by certain bowing difficulties, notably in playing spiccato, caused by rheumatism, and commendably opted to withdraw from concert life rather than allow his public to detect the onset of imperfections. Subsequently, he played only for a few special occasions.

In December 1935 the Decca Record Company had made a highly successful first recording of Walton's new work, his First Symphony. In October 1937 Decca wrote to inform OUP that it was now planning to record the Viola Concerto and to ask OUP to reserve the first recording rights.[22] The obvious soloist would have been Tertis, but his unswerving idealism may not have allowed him to respond to a Decca invitation after having announced his official retirement.

The viola player Frederick Riddle (1913–1995) was a valued member of the London Symphony Orchestra and was shortly (in 1938) to become Beecham's principal viola in his recently formed London Philharmonic Orchestra. Riddle received a telephone call from Lionel Tertis asking if he had a copy of the concerto.[23] Riddle said he would get one, and some ten days later he found himself giving a studio broadcast with the composer conducting. On 6 December 1937, Riddle and Walton met again at the Decca Studios in Thames Street, London, to make the first recording of the concerto with the London Symphony Orchestra.[24] The resulting set of records played an important part in establishing the concerto's secure place in the repertory.

William Primrose recorded Walton's Viola Concerto twice: first in 1946 with the Philharmonia Orchestra and the composer,[25] and second in 1955 with the Royal Philharmonic Orchestra under Sir Malcolm Sargent.[26] To date, the concerto has also been recorded by Paul Doktor, Yehudi Menuhin, Peter Schidlof, Nigel Kennedy, Nobuko Imai, Yuri Bashmet, and Lars Anders Tomter.

Walton's two orchestrations

The brilliant but challenging content and scoring of *Portsmouth Point* and the First Orchestral Suite from *Façade* promoted the general view of Walton as something of an *enfant terrible*; the lyrical idiom and subtle scoring of his Viola Concerto caused the image to be reassessed. The 1929 orchestration calls for triple woodwind, four horns, three trumpets, three trombones, and tuba, timpani, and strings. This seems a large orchestra to accompany a solo instrument whose tone is rich rather than penetrating and which is pitched mainly in the middle register, but it can be observed that the full orchestra is reserved for the tutti passages only and the forces called for are in fact there to provide a full palette of instrumental colour. Walton has also carefully specified in the score that the string desks should be reduced to 4.3.2.2.1 when the solo viola is playing. In an article previewing Tertis's 60th-birthday concert, the 32-year-old Constant Lambert wrote astutely of Walton's orchestration of this work:

Although the composer has not scrupled to use a full modern orchestra, the problem of the balance between soloist and orchestra has been most skilfully solved. While the soloist is playing the strings are … reduced to a few desks only, so that practically speaking the work is scored for two orchestras: a chamber orchestra during the solos and full orchestra during the tuttis. Apart from this the composer has had the intelligence to realize that what covers up a solo string instrument is not so much the brass as the other strings. On paper one would think trombones and trumpets too heavy an accompaniment for a solo viola, but in practice they are so different in tone that the solo instrument stands out clearly against their superior power.[27]

Nevertheless over the years Walton introduced several minor changes of detail by way of revision and refinement, and rather more major ones in 1955. These modifications, clearly shown in an OUP reference score and entered into the orchestral parts by copyists, have been incorporated in the present edition of the original version.

In 1961 Walton wrote to OUP to say that he had decided to re-score the concerto. The new orchestration specifies double woodwind instead of triple, only two trumpets and no tuba, and a harp part is added. The string desks to accompany the solo passages are shown as 4.3.3.2.2. Walton's letter to OUP dated 16 October 1961 states, 'It is I think an improvement on the old version particularly as regards clarity and definition'; his reasons for undertaking this re-scoring do not appear to be documented anywhere else. In a letter of 7 September 1961 he had written to Alan Frank: 'I agree about the Viola Concerto, that the new version need not cancel out the original—it just may be on occasion more convenient.' The word 'Reduced' appears in blue crayon on the first page of the 1961 autograph, and the revised score is sometimes referred to as the 'reduced version', which suggests that the smaller orchestra required may have also been intended to encourage more performances. The new orchestration received its first performance on 18 January 1962, with John Coulling as soloist and the London Philharmonic Orchestra under Sir Malcolm Sargent. It was published in study score format in 1964.

It has always been assumed that Walton's purpose in re-scoring the concerto was to lighten the texture in the interests of balance with the solo line, but closer examination shows that this is scarcely the case. An additional desk of violas and of double basses is prescribed in the solo sections and the woodwind frequently sounds thicker than before, since the second oboe part is scored for cor anglais throughout and the second clarinet frequently takes bass clarinet. (The loss of third trumpet and tuba does not affect the solo part, as they play only in tutti sections in the 1929 orchestration.) Walton's extensive use of the harp in his 1962 score suggests that he had by then evolved a different orchestral sound; the harp is used conspicuously in his scores for Laurence Olivier's three Shakespeare films and also the opera *Troilus and Cressida*. But the new version was not to everybody's taste. A review by Ronald Crichton in the *Financial Times* of Walton's 70th-birthday concert at the Royal Festival Hall, in which Yehudi Menuhin was the soloist in the Viola Concerto, made a perceptive comment: 'one wished that just this once they had gone back to the old scoring with triple wind and without harp—no doubt the revisions make life easier for the solo, but the smoothing and streamlining tone down an acerbity that was very much part of the music, while the harp brings it nearer the Tennysonian euphony of Ischia and the later period, very beautiful, yet different'.[28]

The 'Koussevitsky' version

A certain mystery surrounds an alternative autograph of the 1929 score, which surfaced when the Library of Congress was bequeathed the library of the celebrated conductor Serge Koussevitsky in 1978. A letter from Walton to Koussevitsky in Boston dated 30 December 1929 (just under three months after the première) states, 'I have sent to you under separate cover the score of my Viola Concerto, also a part for the player. I am so sorry that I have been unable to send it before, but my publishers insisted on its going to press, and so I have only just had the score returned to me. The parts will arrive in Boston by the end of the month. Thank you so much for giving the work its first American performance, and I only hope that it meets with your approval'. Koussevitsky's reply of 8 February 1930 to Walton in Amalfi acknowledges receipt of score and viola part.[29]

In April 1982 the Library of Congress returned this autograph score to OUP in London, and it is now part of the Frederick R. Koch Collection in Yale.[30] What is mysterious about it is that it shows certain differences from the main autograph which formed the basis for the first printed edition. It is written on larger paper, so that each woodwind instrument has its own stave throughout, and it shows numerous changes of notation, slurs, and dynamics, as well as a few errors. The most immediately striking difference is found at the very opening which, in this version, begins *pianissimo* with a crescendo for first violins and violas until a *subito pianissimo* at the moment of the soloist's first entry. In four passages several bars of the solo part have been changed, then heavily crossed out and the notes reinstated as in the printed score. The number of string desks prescribed for the solo passages is 4.3.2.2.2, which allows one more desk of double basses than is required in the 1930 publication.[31] It must be broadly contemporary with the main autograph, since the opening theme of the finale is scored for two clarinets and bass clarinet—which had already become two bassoons by the time the printed full score and piano arrangement were published in 1930. The second and third movements show blue crayon conductor's markings (tricky changes of metre in large figures). Did this autograph simply represent an alternative version (especially at the opening it has the look of a neat fair copy) or is it perhaps an earlier score to which the main autograph is a more practical successor? And why, having said that he had waited for the return of the autograph score, would Walton send a *different* version for the first American performance? Mysterious.

The solo line

The soloists in the concerto's early performances played from manuscript—Paul Hindemith at the première in October 1929 and Bernard Shore in the 1930 Promenade Concert with the newly formed BBC Symphony Orchestra, of which he was principal viola.[32] The solo line shown in the arrangement for viola and piano, of 1930, agreed with that of the published full score. The present edition of the 1929 version gives this line on the smaller stave. The full-sized stave gives a version of the solo line whose provenance is slightly more complicated.

When Frederick Riddle played the work for his studio broadcast and the first recording he devised different phrasings and bowings—without changing the actual notes—and the composer is known to have found these changed articulations an improvement on the previously published ones, both his own and the Tertis version. He therefore asked Riddle to submit his edition of the solo part to OUP for publication. The existing plates were altered (a bill for £6 18s 6d from the printers is dated 13 May 1938), and the Riddle version was put on sale with the piano reduction, though for some reason Riddle's name was not credited. It remained the only version of the solo line available with the piano reduction until the appearance of the revised orchestration in 1962.

Unfortunately, when Walton was making his new orchestration in 1961 a major misunderstanding caused a change to the published solo part which the composer did not intend. Before undertaking his re-orchestration he had written to OUP asking them to prepare a dummy score in which he could enter the new instrumentation. A copyist was to draw the barlines and enter the instrument names and the viola solo line; all other staves were to remain blank. The dummy score was duly prepared, and Walton used it to create his new orchestration.[33] However, the solo line that had been copied into the score was from the 1930 published full score, that is to say the version that had been superseded by Riddle's version. Walton somewhat confused the issue by entering into the (incorrect) solo line of this score a few alternatives ('8va', 'con 8va', etc.) derived from Primrose's ideas, possibly for his own experimental purposes.

And yet he had clearly been worried by the text of the solo part that he had been given, for a letter to him from Alan Frank of OUP, dated 29 September 1961, states 'I am not quite sure what you mean by "other versions of the solo part". But since what you have in the dummy score was copied from the [1930] printed score, maybe this printed solo part is of some help'. The card that Walton enclosed when sending OUP the new MS score read, 'I take it that all three Viola parts agree—the Pfte. [arrangement] and full score *and the solo part as revised by Riddle*' (italics added). This was not understood by OUP, who replied on 31 May 1963, 'We decided that there ought to be one solo viola part for use with both orchestrations. When the reprinted copies of the piano score arrive—which will be quite soon—the inserted [i.e. separate] viola solo part will agree with the viola part in the new score'. Note OUP's reference to the score, Walton's to the part. To take the viola line from the full score would normally be correct, but OUP had forgotten that the solo line of the 1930 publication had been replaced by Riddle's 1938 version with the composer's approval—and we find Walton writing on 13 June 1963, 'The printed part which I returned with the proofs is the one revised by Fred Riddle and the one I did ask to be used for the new version'.

It was, however, too late. OUP had unfortunately allowed the wrong solo line to be copied into the specially prepared dummy score into which Walton had entered his new orchestration, and the composer seems to have realized this at a point when the misunderstanding could not be rectified. As a result, the solo part put on sale with the piano reduction from 1963 until the present day has been derived from the long-abandoned original 1930 solo part, with some thirty added instructions and changes. The solo line shown in the William Walton Edition is the one that the composer made abundantly clear he wanted, namely Frederick Riddle's version.

Although Walton admired the virtuoso performances given by Tertis and Primrose, and although Lionel Tertis's edition of the solo line had been available for some years, when it came to deciding on a text it was Riddle's disciplined and balanced approach that he ultimately favoured.

The Riddle version

Frederick Riddle's revision of the 1930 solo part is admired by viola players—as presumably it was by the composer—for two special qualities. First, the phrasings and articulations convey the nature of the work even more successfully than the original, and second, they achieve solutions to technical problems caused not only by legitimate musical requirements but also by the young composer's admitted lack of knowledge of his solo instrument. If we compare, for instance, the two solo lines shown in the present edition at the opening of the 1929 score we can see how Riddle's version succeeds in bringing out the lyrical and nostalgic character of the first statement and at the same time organizes the bowings to deliver the soloist to the appropriate part of the bow (bars 4–22). Grouping the viola's accompanying octaves in threes rather than the original pairs in bars 13–14, and also 17–18, is slightly more tranquil, less distracting. Conversely, the fourth bar of the second movement gains from Riddle's separating the first three notes and linking the fourth and fifth: the attack is crisp and the bow kept near the strongest part, at the heel, while in Walton's original the slur on the first three notes uses more bow length so that the two staccato notes have to be played less suitably further up the bow.

These are simple, isolated examples of the many changes to be found in the Riddle version. Some of them are quite small, but in detail and in perspective they add technical expertise and a stylish dimension to the writing. Riddle's playing for that broadcast and recording must have impressed Walton as being sufficiently convincing for him to encourage the immediate publication of his soloist's reworking as the version of his choice.

Just as it is clear from Walton's correspondence that he preferred Riddle's revision of the solo part, it also emerges from successive letters that his belief in his 1962 orchestration grew; from initially regarding it as a simple alternative to the 1929 score he eventually favoured it outright.[34] On the other hand, referring to the Sinfonia Concertante, first performed in 1928 but revised in 1943, Walton told his cataloguer Stewart Craggs in 1978 that he thought the original version was 'better and more interesting'.[35] Since 1962 many musicians have expressed a preference for the fuller 1929 orchestration of the concerto, among them Sir Malcolm Sargent, Norman Del Mar, and Michael Kennedy, all of whom would have been accustomed to the 1938 recording. It seems appropriate to point out that both scores have their individual merits; the 1929 score, which established the concerto's original impact and reputation, and the 1962 revision, which prescribes a somewhat smaller orchestra and reflects the composer's later preferences in instrumentation.

Whichever version is performed, William Walton's Concerto for Viola and Orchestra is surely established as a classic of the twentieth century and a major pinnacle of the viola repertory.

CHRISTOPHER WELLINGTON
Southbourne, 2001

ENDNOTES

1 *Musical News and Herald*, 27 May 1922.
2 Lionel Tertis, *My Viola and I* (London, 1974), pp. 16, 18. This is the revised and enlarged edition of his 1953 original, *Cinderella No More*.
3 The correspondence with Sassoon is preserved at the William Walton Museum, Forio, Ischia.
4 *RCM Magazine*, Vol. 80, No. 3, p. 123.
5 'Walton in the 20s', *BBC Music Magazine*, 26 March 1972.
6 For further discussion of these influences, see Robert Meikle, 'The Symphonies and Concertos' in Stewart Craggs, ed., *William Walton: Music and Literature* (Aldershot, 1999), pp. 70–74.
7 Tertis, *My Viola and I*, p. 36.
8 Conversation with Christopher Wellington.
9 Susana Walton, *Behind the Façade* (Oxford, 1988), pp. 34–5.
10 Bernard Shore, *Sixteen Symphonies* (London, 1949), p. 367.
11 Geoffrey Skelton, ed. and trans., *Selected Letters of Paul Hindemith* (New Haven, CT, 1995), p. 54.
12 *The Times*, 4 October 1929.
13 *Musical Times*, 70, 1 November 1929, p. 1030.
14 Geoffrey Skelton, *Paul Hindemith: the Man behind the Music* (London, 1975), p. 98. Walton told Skelton of his awareness of Hindemith's *Kammermusik Nr. 5* and, referring to the première of his own viola concerto, added 'I was surprised he played it. One or two bars are almost identical.'
15 Tertis, *My Viola and I*, pp. 36–7. The need for a large viola was an article of faith with Tertis; any player whose viola measured less than 16½ inches (41.9 cm.), length of back, was liable to be told, 'Put it on the fire, my boy—that's all it's fit for!'
16 *A Bundle of Time: The Memoirs of Harriet Cohen* (London, 1969), p. 169.
17 Tertis, *My Viola and I*, p. 71.
18 A letter of 13 November 1975 from Thomas Russell (a former secretary and business manager of the LPO) to Walton states, 'Soon after your Concerto for Viola and Orchestra was presented I acquired a copy of the solo part edited by Lionel Tertis. In 1932 or soon after I studied the work with him', OUP Archive, Oxford.
19 Walton was always receptive to practical advice; as late as 1982 Rostropovitch edited the first publication of the Passacaglia for cello solo.
20 OUP Archive; all the correspondence cited between Walton and OUP is from the same source.
21 29 April 1964, OUP Archive.
22 Letter from the Decca Record Co. of 8 October 1937, OUP Archive.
23 Conversation with Christopher Wellington.
24 Decca X 199–201. Remastered for CD by Dutton Laboratories in 1993 on 'Walton Gramophone Premières' (with Symphony No. I and Three Songs from *Façade*), CDAX 8003. It is sometimes incorrectly stated that the recording was made in Kingsway Hall.
25 HMV AB6309–11 (autochange version DB9036–8); reissued in 1996 on CD in a William Primrose collection, Pearl GEMM CD9252.
26 Philips ABL 3045 (mono).
27 *The Listener*, 17 February 1937.
28 *Financial Times*, 30 March 1972. Quoted by Michael Kennedy in *Portrait of Walton* (Oxford, 1989), p. 251.
29 Both letters in OUP Archive.
30 Beinecke Rare Book and Manuscript Library, Yale University.
31 The RCM autograph, which acted as printer's copy for the first publication, also prescribes two desks of basses.
32 Shore's performance was on 21 August 1930, with Walton conducting. Talking about the composition of the concerto in a BBC interview with John Amis on 4 June 1977 Walton acknowledged that 'I had a sort of help from Bernard Shore'.
33 This manuscript was photographed by OUP and several copies made for use as hire conducting scores until the new orchestration was eventually published in 1964.
34 An OUP instruction to the Hire Department of 25 February 1969 reads, 'If anyone specifies the old version please advise them first that the composer infinitely prefers the new version'. OUP Archive.
35 Kennedy, *Portrait of Walton*, p. 45.

To Christabel
Concerto for Viola and Orchestra
I

Viola part revised by
Frederick Riddle
Piano reduction by
Geoffrey Pratley

WILLIAM WALTON

4

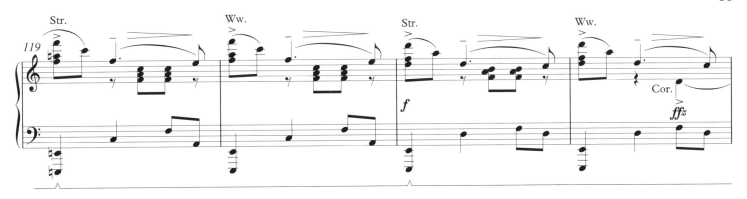

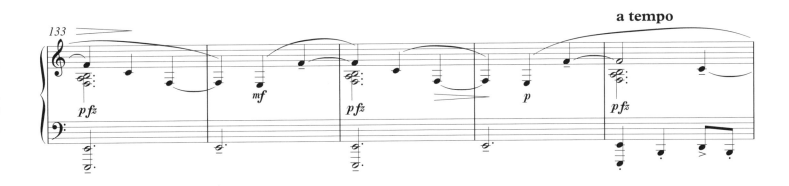

II

Vivo e molto preciso ♩ = *c.*116
♩ = *c.*144–152

16

★) ossia:

24

★) ossia:

III

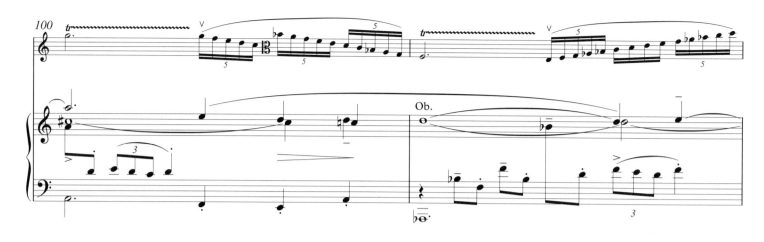

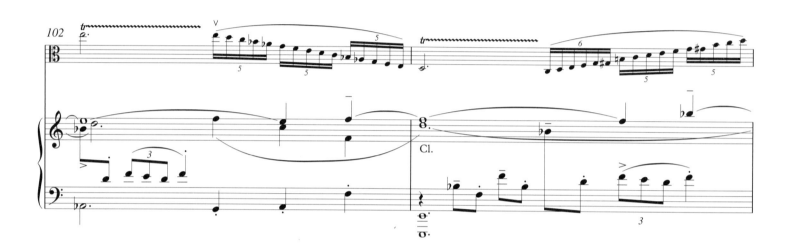

poco rall.

A tempo più mosso (♩ = c.84)

47

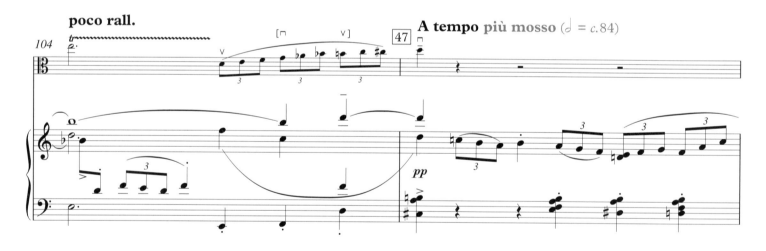

poco accel.

a tempo

40

Più mosso poco a poco

Più mosso (𝅗𝅥 = c.108)

Poco largamente   **Allargamente** ($\sonata = c.84$)
rit.

poco rit.   **più allarg.** ($\sonata = c.80$)

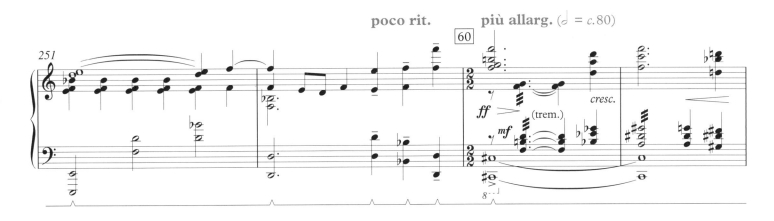

a tempo

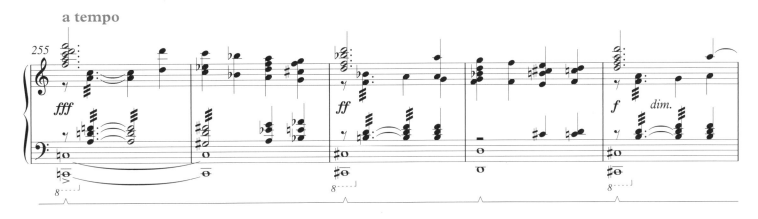

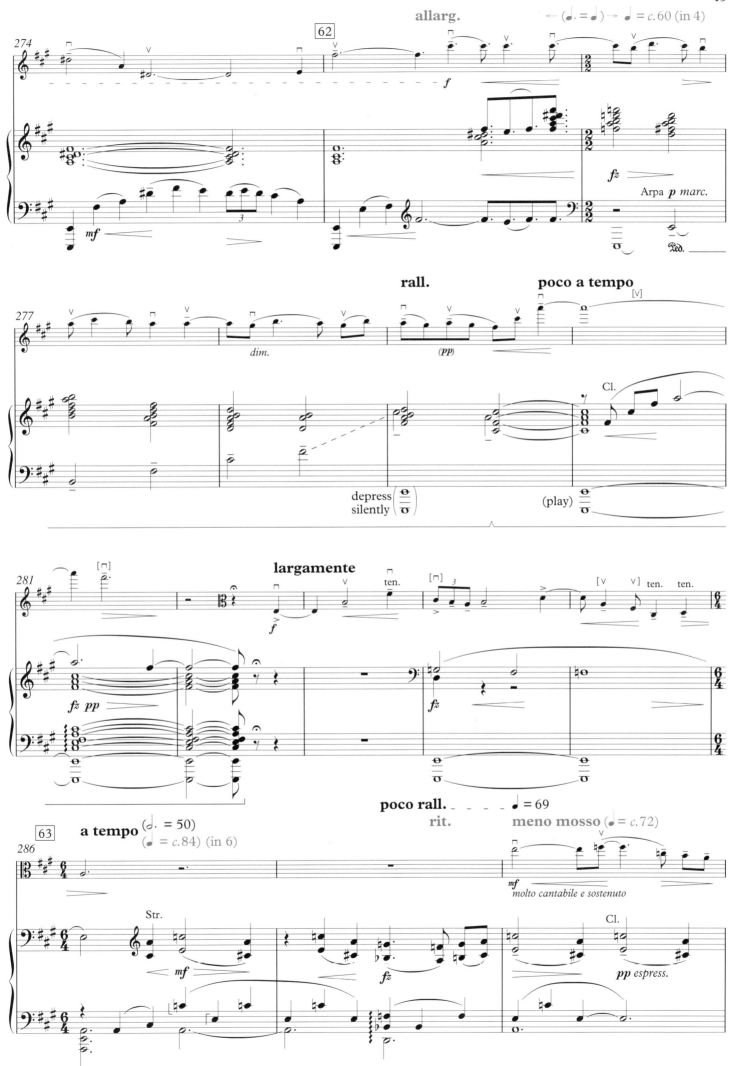